THE TRUE STORY BEHIND ALFRED HITCHCOCK'S PSYCHO

Stranger Than Fiction Series Book #1

FERGUS MASON

Absolute Crime Press
ANAHEIM, CALIFORNIA

Copyright © 2020 by Golgotha Press, Inc.

All rights reserved. No part of this publication may be reproduced, distributed or transmitted in any form or by any means, including photocopying, recording, or other electronic or mechanical methods, without the prior written permission of the publisher, except in the case of brief quotations embodied in critical reviews and certain other noncommercial uses permitted by copyright law.

Limited Liability / Disclaimer of Warranty. While best efforts have been used in preparing this book, the author and publishers make no representations or warranties of any kind and assume no liabilities of any kind with respect to accuracy or completeness of the content and specifically the author nor publisher shall be held liable or responsible to any person or entity with respect to any loss or incidental or consequential damages caused or alleged to have been caused, directly, or indirectly without limitations, by the information or programs contained herein. Furthermore, readers should be aware that the Internet sites listed in this work may have changed or disappeared. This work is sold with the understanding that the advice inside may not be suitable in every situation.

Trademarks. Where trademarks are used in this book this infers no endorsement or any affiliation with this book. Any trademarks (including, but not limiting to, screenshots) used in this book are solely used for editorial and educational purposes.

Contents

About Absolute Crime..7

Introduction..9

Genesis of a Monster..14

The Real Buffalo Bill..27

House of Horrors...35

Thinking About Norman...41

Challenging Hollywood..49

Creating the Plot...53

Shooting Begins..59

Creating the Horror..66

Reception..74

Conclusion..79

Ready for More?...83

    The True Story Behind Alfred Hitchcock's The Birds 83

    Exposing Jack the Stripper: A Biography of the Worst Serial Killer You've Probably Never Heard Of.......... 84

    The Sapphire Affair: The True Story Behind Alfred Hitchcock's Topaz.. 84

    The Perfect Crime: The Real Life Crime that Inspired Hitchcock's Rope 85

    The True Story Behind Alfred Hitchcock's The Wrong Man 86

Newsletter Offer 87

About Absolute Crime

Absolute Crime publishes only the best true crime literature. Our focus is on the crimes that you've probably never heard of, but you are fascinated to read more about. With each engaging and gripping story, we try to let readers relive moments in history that some people have tried to forget.

Remember, our books are not meant for the faint at heart. We don't hold back--if a crime is bloody, we let the words splatter across the page so you can experience the crime in the most horrifying way!

If you enjoy this book, please visit our homepage (www.AbsoluteCrime.com) to see other books we offer; if you have any feedback, we'd love to hear from you!

Sign up for our mailing list, and we'll send you out a free true crime book!
http://www.absolutecrime.com/newsletter

Introduction

For movie buffs Alfred Hitchcock will always be associated with a long list of Hollywood classics. Between 1921 and 1976 the English director known as the Master of Suspense released 52 feature films, many of which are still thrilling new audiences today. To most people, though, he's best known for a film that was very different – Psycho.

As his nickname suggests most of Hitchcock's movies are tightly plotted and intricate, using ingenious plot twists to keep viewers guessing until the last moment. Big budgets and glamorous scenery made his films as visually stunning as they were psychologically ingenious. Then, in 1959, he did something completely new. Intrigued by the low-budget horror titles that were being produced by small independents outside the Hollywood studio system he decided to see how good one could be if a director of his talents was involved.

His plot idea came from a newly published horror novel loosely inspired by one of the most gruesome crimes of the 1950s, the tale of a small-town grave robber and murderer who turned female bodies into grotesque homeware articles and freakish clothing. Hollywood wasn't interested in the book. Such sensationalist – not to say gory – material was beneath them, and the studio executives thought it wouldn't bring in the audiences. Hitchcock thought they were wrong, and with his trademark single-mindedness he set out to prove it.

Through the end of winter 1959 and into the early summer of 1960 Hitchcock worked in a small TV production lot outside the hub of Hollywood. As industry moguls shook their heads in reproach he surrounded himself with his own production crew, taken from his TV show, and talked a small group of talented actors and actresses into risking their careers on a violent, morally ambiguous shocker. Tight security sealed his lot off from the curious press, until in late May he threw the doors open and invited the cameras in for a tantalizing trailer that he narrated himself. In the meantime he had overcome technical challenges, budget problems and the suspicion of the movie censors, who had battled with him over scenes showing fornication, murder and – weirdly – bathroom fittings.

By early June the movie-going public was eager to learn what all the mystery was about. The film critics were less thrilled. Denied the advance screenings they felt their exalted status entitled them to, they sneered at Hitchcock's antics and predicted disaster for the movie. When the doors opened and they joined the public in front of the screen their reviews were faintly damning. Not Hitchcock's best, the critics agreed. Unsubtle, a gimmick and in bad taste.

The audiences didn't agree. They loved it, and flocked to see it in millions. By the end of the year it was the highest-grossing film of Hitchcock's career and the most profitable black and white movie of all time. Even today it remains popular; three sequels and a TV spinoff have been made and it even earned the dubious honor of a modern remake (which flopped.)

For Hollywood, Psycho changed the rules. The Prohibition-era censorship that set boundaries for the movie industry had been under strain for years and was being routinely bypassed by independents and foreign imports. Now one of the giants of the industry had driven a bulldozer straight through it. Within a few years it had crumbled away completely and been replaced by the modern rating system. The success of Psycho opened the way for a flood of low-budget shockers, but it also left the road clear for classics of suspense horror like Halloween and Silence of the Lambs.

Psycho hit the screen in June of 1960 and dominated theaters for the rest of the year. It was one of the first defining events of the sixties, challenging taboos about sex and violence that had never been seriously questioned before. It's remarkable that it all began years earlier in a tiny, conventional Wisconsin village.

[1]
GENESIS OF A MONSTER

For any director looking to make a suspense movie, serial killers are an obvious choice. Most homicides are one-offs, committed in the heat of the moment by a killer who makes little effort to cover their tracks afterwards. In fact many of them, stricken with remorse, call the police right away to confess. You'd never guess it from Hollywood but the words a homicide detective hears most often are probably "I didn't mean to kill him." These squalid little everyday crimes don't have a lot of box office appeal, but serial killers are something else. Motivated and remorseless, using intricate planning or animal cunning to evade capture and stalk their next victim, the knowledge that they'll kill and kill again until stopped gives huge potential to build suspense.

Fictional serial killers stalk many classic movies, including Dirty Harry, Halloween, The Hitcher and the Nightmare on Elm Street franchise. Real-life killers have also been immortalized on film – the Son of Sam, Henry Lucas, the Zodiac Killer and many more have inspired directors and horrified audiences.

The murderer who's had the biggest influence on Hollywood, though, may not even have been a serial killer. He was convicted of a single murder and confessed to a second, although some people believe he may have committed at least another six and there's plenty of circumstantial evidence to back that up. Even one murder is an appalling crime, but compared with the toll of John Wayne Gacy (at least 34 victims), Ted Bundy (at least 36) or Green River Killer Gary Ridgway (more than 90) he was strictly small-time. Despite that the grotesque nature of his crimes inspired some of the best known villains in cinema, including Leatherface in the Texas Chainsaw Massacre series, Buffalo Bill in The Silence of the Lambs and the most famous movie murderer of them all – crazed motel owner Norman Bates.

If somebody wanted to illustrate the melting pot idea of American immigration they'd be hard pressed to find a better example than Wisconsin. At one time or another just about every wave of immigration to the USA has washed over the state. The one that's had most influence on it crested in the late 19th century, when hundreds of thousands of Germans flooded into the growing industrial towns. These hard-working newcomers, mostly from Prussia and Westphalia, settled in well and devoted their energies to succeeding in their new land. They clung to elements of their old identity though; German was often spoken at home, and it took a generation or two for the names of their children to become Anglicized and most of them stayed within the religion they'd brought with them, the Lutheran Church.

In July 1878 Augusta Wilhelmina Lehrke was born to two of these immigrants in Waushura County. Her middle name was a tribute to the first German Emperor, who had been proclaimed seven years before, and reflected her parents' pride in their Prussian ancestry. She was also brought up in the Lutheran faith. As a young woman she married local man George Philip Gein, who was also of German descent, but the marriage quickly ran into difficulties. George had alcohol problems and found it difficult to hold a job, and although the couple had two sons Augusta increasingly despised her husband. Their first child, Henry, was born in 1901. The second, Edward Theodore Gein, followed on August 27, 1906. To support them George worked at a variety of jobs, including carpentry and selling insurance, while Augusta ran a small grocery store in the town of La Crosse. The store provided most of the family's income and George's irregular earnings mostly ended up being spent on alcohol. Augusta, a strong personality, became increasingly overbearing thanks to her role as breadwinner and effective head of the family. This was to have a terrible effect on her younger son. A shy child who didn't feel comfortable in social situations, Edward was steadily warped by his mother's dominating behavior until a quiet but good-natured boy had been transformed into a monster.

Along with her growing self-importance and sense of superiority, Augusta's personality was also being transformed by her religious views. The German Lutheran faith is an undemonstrative one, mostly concerned with promoting the virtues of hard work and a Prussian sense of good order and thrift. In Augusta's case the spirit of the times was changing it into something very different. Scholars of American Christianity sometimes call the period from about 1850 to the USA's entry into the First World War "the Third Great Awakening." In these decades the country generated a huge number of campaigning pastors, mostly from Protestant sects and mostly concerned with social reform. The Temperance movement that led to Prohibition had its roots in this phenomenon, as did the late 19th century surge in missionary activity, but it had positive effects too – crusading church groups pushed for many reforms to child labor laws, women's suffrage and the emancipation of slaves, as well as founding many of America's leading universities.

These reforms all came out of a muscular, justice-driven Protestantism of the "hard work and cold baths" school of thought, but the Great Awakening energized other sorts of preachers, too. Especially in the Midwest millions of people listened to tent revivalists and prophets of Armageddon. Some of them were little more than con men who used the Bible as a prop; others were genuinely crazy. Augusta Gein seems to have spent too long listening to the second type. As her sons grew up she became increasingly obsessed with sin and degeneracy, a fixation that worked its way into the insults she threw at her husband. Her views of society also began to change. America, she started to believe, was a cesspool of immorality and vice (in fact it was then, as it is today, easily the most devout of the western industrial nations.) More and more her thoughts turned to protecting herself and her sons from the corruption that would inevitably infect them without her intervention.[1]

Augusta believed that society was corrupt, so it was essential to insulate her family from society as much as possible. In 1914 she sold her grocery store and used the money to buy a 195-acre farm outside Plainfield. The closest neighbors were a quarter of a mile away and the boys were forbidden from having much contact with them. Edward, only eight years old, found himself cut off from the outside world; he left the farm only to go to school, where his shyness made it difficult for him to make friends. If he ever did show signs of forming a friendship with another boy he was punished by his mother. He was upset by this, but he worshipped Augusta and tried his best to comply with her stern rules.

It didn't make a lot of difference how much he tried to please her though; Augusta was never satisfied with the boys' behavior and frequently humiliated them, telling them they would grow up to be useless alcoholics like their father. Outcast at school and strictly controlled at home, young Ed's upbringing was almost calculated to do as much psychological damage as possible. By removing practically all interactions with other people Augusta made herself into the center of her younger son's life. Henry, seven years older, had had a chance to develop more of a normal personality before the family shut themselves away outside Plainfield and he was finding his mother's regime frustrating.

George Gein died of alcohol-related heart failure in April 1940, reducing the family's already modest income. To help make ends meet Henry and Ed started working as odd job men around the town. Locals found them both to be hard working and trustworthy. Henry had a strong work ethic and Ed, who idolized his big brother – the only male company he had after his father's death – wanted to emulate him. Now both in their thirties, the Gein brothers continued in their strange, semi-isolated existence. Mostly they worked as handymen, but if there were a few dollars in it they'd turn their hands to just about anything. One surprising source of income was babysitting. Ed seemed to have a gift for it – in fact he got on better with children than he did with the adults he encountered. Looking back this is hardly surprising, because his mother's tyrannical influence had deprived him of the skills he needed to relate to people and he was frozen in a child-like state of emotional development. The details of life on the Gein farm were far beyond the understanding of Ed's neighbors though, and they were just grateful that they could rely on him to take care of their kids occasionally.

Henry was better at getting along with people, and he was also growing concerned at the depth of Augusta's domination of his younger brother. He felt it wasn't natural for a grown man to have no adult companionship except for his mother, and he feared that Ed's worship of her couldn't end well. He had no idea how right he was.

With George dead, Augusta's horizons had narrowed even more and her only priority was keeping her sons pure and free from the corruption she imagined all around her, while at the same time reminding them that they were also doomed to disgrace and condemnation. Life under these circumstances was too claustrophobic for Henry to cope with. Sometime after his father's death he began seeing a local woman, a divorcee with two young children. The relationship steadily progressed and around 1943 he began talking about moving out of the farm and living with her. Ed was appalled. How could his beloved brother even contemplate something so sinful? And what would Mother think?

Henry Gein didn't care what Mother would think. In fact he had a few things to say about Mother, none of them very flattering. Ed was shocked to hear this blasphemy. That didn't stop Henry though. As time went on he became more and more critical of Augusta and the way she tried to control every aspect of their lives. As long as he could remember Henry had been Ed's idol, second only to his beloved mother. Now tension started to mount between the brothers, with Ed's outrage on one side and Henry's increasing frustration on the other. Thanks to the family's isolation it's hard to know exactly how bad that tension got, but given what happened next we can guess.

Some of the land on the Gein farm was damp and marshy, and thick, choking brush tended to spread out from it onto better soil.

Every so often it had to be cleared and the Geins did that by burning. On May 16, 1944 the brothers were burning off a patch when the flames started spreading out of control. The Plainfield fire department noticed the blaze and turned out to help, and by evening the flames were out. The firefighters returned to their homes, but Henry Gein did not. Just before nightfall Ed reported his brother missing. The police quickly put together a search party and headed out to the farm. Much to their surprise Ed led them straight to Henry. He wasn't missing; he was dead.

There were enough questions about how Henry had died to cause suspicion. The patch of ground his body was lying on hadn't burned, so an autopsy was possible. While it found that he had died of asphyxiation, it also turned up bruises on his head.[2] Nobody could believe foul play was involved though. Ed was well known in the town as a strange but harmless character, and the police were happy to accept the death as an accident. Asphyxiation from smoke inhalation is the leading cause of death around fires and it's easy enough to bruise your head falling down. As for the unburned ground, it's natural for anyone caught in a fire to head for a place that isn't burning. Henry was buried and life at the increasingly strange farm went on.

Ed was now alone with his mother, who seemed to be all the company he needed. Things were going downhill though. Not long after Henry died Augusta, who was now in her late sixties and had been living under a high level of self-induced stress for most of her life, suffered a stroke. It wasn't fatal but it left her partially paralyzed. That increased the workload for Ed, who now had to care for her as well as running the struggling farm and doing enough handyman work to bring in a steady income. For someone as socially inept as him it was too much to handle.

On December 29, 1945 Augusta Gein died soon after suffering a second stroke, apparently brought on by realizing that another local farmer was living with a woman he wasn't married to. Ed was devastated by the loss. His mother had been almost the only adult company he'd known, and was the only woman he'd ever had a close relationship with. Up to now his life had run along a course that she'd marked out for him and, however eccentric that journey was, he'd been making it under close and strict supervision. Now he was on his own. It was only a matter of time before he went shockingly off the rails.

[2]
THE REAL BUFFALO BILL

People disappear all the time, especially in America. It's a big country with a mobile population, after all. In Europe it was common, even two generations ago, for someone to live their entire life in a ten-mile radius with only occasional trips outside of it for vacations. The USA has always been different. Maybe because of the nation's pioneer history people are a lot more willing to strike out for somewhere new, and start over again in a different state. Often they'd just as soon not hear from anyone connected to their old life – especially creditors – so they might not be all that diligent about leaving a forwarding address or even announcing their departure. Most missing person reports turn out to be people who've just had enough and moved on. Not all, though. In among the disappeared are some who've fallen victim to serial killers.

The American Midwest has a lot to offer, but for many young people it lacks the glamor of the coasts and inevitably some of them opt for a change of scenery. Police in Wisconsin are used to a certain number of unsolved disappearances every year. In the late 1940s and 1950s they noticed a sudden increase in missing persons around Plainfield. The string of strange incidents, all of them in or near the small town, was enough to get their attention. Some of them were truly baffling. In May 1947 an eight-year-old girl, Georgia Weckler, set out to walk home from school in Jefferson and was never seen again. Victor Travis and Ray Burgess stopped for a few beers at a Plainfield bar in November 1952, got back in their car and vanished. In 1953 Evelyn Hartley was abducted from a La Crosse home where she'd been babysitting, leaving behind her spectacles, a shoe and some bloodstains. The next year

Mary Hogan disappeared from the tavern she ran in Plainfield; a blood trail led out into the parking lot and a single spent .22 shell case lay on the floor. After each incident searches were organized and investigations launched – especially in the cases of Hartley and Hogan, where there were signs of foul play. None of the efforts led anywhere though. It was obvious that something terrible was going on but the meager clues didn't point to a suspect. Then Plainfield storeowner Bernice Worden vanished.

On November 15, 1957 Ed Gein had dropped in at Worden's hardware store and spoken to her and her son. He'd asked for a gallon of antifreeze and said he'd collect it the next day. After Worden vanished the next day her receipt pad was found in the store and the last receipt she'd written was for a gallon of antifreeze. That was enough for the investigators to decide it was worth talking to Gein; it strongly suggested that he'd seen her on the day of her disappearance and perhaps he could shed some light on what had happened. The local police had an incentive to find Bernice

Worden quickly because her son Frank was a sheriff's deputy.

Arriving at the Gein farm on the 17th the Plainfield sheriff, Arthur Schley, was horrified at the squalid scene they discovered. Some rooms of the farmhouse had been boarded up; the others were indescribably filthy, cluttered with junk and heaps of stinking garbage. The sole occupant seemed to live in the kitchen and a small room that opened off it, and his existence was almost subhuman. The smell was nauseating, a thick stench of dirt and decay. Stacks of lurid magazines were everywhere – pulp shockers filled with tales of cannibalism, Nazism and bizarre murders. Schley had probably gone out to the farm to interview Gein about his visit to the store the previous day, but now he decided it might be a good idea to search the farm. The degeneration he'd found there suggested something a lot more sinister than a sad loner who missed his mother.

While his deputies rummaged through the mess in the house Schley set out to explore the decrepit outbuildings. Opening the door of a shed he clicked on his flashlight and gingerly advanced into the stinking interior. Then he felt something brush his shoulder. Turning, he raised the light – then recoiled in horror. Hanging from the roof was a hideously mutilated carcass.

The sight that greeted Schley made sense to anyone who hunted deer, and in Waushara County hunting was popular. The body had been strung from the rafters upside down, the head removed and the abdomen slit open. The entrails had been removed, leaving a gaping cavity. This wasn't a white-tailed deer though. It was a 50-year-old woman. Bernice Worden had been found.

Ed Gein was immediately arrested, and the police continued their search of the farm. It soon became clear that Gein was a deeply disturbed individual. The farmhouse was full of human body parts. Mrs. Worden's head was found in a burlap sack with a .22 bullet hole in it – she'd been killed with a single gunshot then, mercifully, butchered after death. Ten more heads were found, all belonging to women and all with the tops of the skulls sawn off. The crown of at least one skull had been turned into a bowl. A shoebox contained nine sets of preserved female genitalia, a pair of lips had been turned into a novelty pull for a window blind and skulls decorated the posts of Gein's bed. A litter of other human body parts included bones, a heart and four noses.

Most gruesome of all was the collection of items made from human skin. During his checkered career George Gein had worked as a tanner for a while, and it looked like Ed had learned a few things from him. Tanning is the process of turning animal skins into leather, and it works on people just as well as cows or pigs. Chair seats had been recovered, and lampshades and a wastepaper basket had been created from human leather. A grotesque belt had been stitched together from tanned nipples. Nine masks made of skin were discovered. Then the appalled officers made the most shocking find of all.

In the movie The Silence of the Lambs FBI agent Starling calls her boss to say that the serial killer is "making himself a girl suit out of real girls." That's exactly what Ed Gein had done.

Gein had stitched together a macabre garment from pieces of tanned female skin. Later he told detectives that he was curious about what it felt like to have breasts and a vagina, so he'd made the suit to find out. He often dreamed of being a woman, he said. This ghoulish dress-up was the closest he could come to that dream.

Maybe the most shocking thing of all was that people in Plainfield had known Gein had a collection of preserved human body parts, even if they hadn't known just how large and gruesome it was. A teenage boy Gein sometimes looked after had visited the farm once and Gein had shown him shrunken heads, which he claimed were mementoes made by South Seas cannibals. The boy had mentioned these revolting artifacts, but nobody had believed him. Later two more teenagers had visited and also seen heads, but thought they were some sort of fancy dress props. After the second incident rumors had started to spread and the townspeople had even joked about Ed's collection of shrunken heads – sometimes to his face. He just smiled and made flippant comments about it. Incredibly, nobody connected these rumors to the spike in missing persons reports.

[3]
House of Horrors

At first Gein confessed only to the killing of Bernice Worden – it would have been hard to deny that, after all, with her slaughtered corpse hanging in his shed. The Plainfield sheriff's department were curious about the other disappearances and tried to get more information out of him, but Gein denied any other murders even when Sheriff Schley lost his temper and smashed his face against the wall. He'd been in a daze when he killed Worden, he said, and couldn't remember all the details. He did remember hauling her body from the hardware store to his old Ford truck, and stealing the cash register. He had no memory of shooting her though.

That left the investigators with a mystery. The sheer number of body parts in the farmhouse meant that even if Gein had been behind all the disappearances there weren't enough corpses to explain them all. When pushed on where the corpses had come from Gein admitted to another crime – grave robbing.

As well as his pulp horror magazines Gein had subscribed to the local newspapers, and one of his favorite reads was the obituary column. From that he learned whenever a local woman had died, and after the funeral – ideally, between burial and the grave being finished – he would drive out to the graveyard after dark, dig down to the coffin, pry it open and steal the corpse. Between 1947 and 1952 he'd made around 40 trips to burial grounds, again in what he called a dazed state. Mostly he'd come out of his fugue before desecrating a grave and just gone home, but on nine occasions he could remember robbing graves. He'd selected women he thought resembled his mother for these thefts; the cadavers had been bundled into his old Ford, taken home and stripped of the parts he wanted. Sometimes he'd gone back to the graves and dug them up yet again, returning what remained of the corpse. Sometimes the unwanted parts had just joined the foul debris in his home. One corpse had been buried on the farm, where police found it on November 29. At first they thought the decayed remains were those of missing deer hunter Victor Travis, but they were later identified as another middle-aged woman whom Gein had excavated and brought home.

Gein was a small, lightly built man and there was some skepticism about his ability to dig up, rob and refill a grave in the course of one night. To settle the argument the State Crime Laboratory got permission to exhume three of the plots Gein had identified. One was empty; one had been disturbed but not robbed, because Gein's pry bar had slipped from his hand and fallen through the wooden grave liner and out of his reach – the rusting tool lay atop the coffin. The third contained body parts and some jewelry, items that Gein had returned after taking what he wanted.

Meanwhile Gein, now under interrogation by the state police, had also admitted to killing Mary Hogan. He couldn't remember what had actually happened, but did recall accidentally shooting her. As Hogan was shot in her own tavern, not a place you'd have expected Gein to have taken his .22 hunting rifle, it was hard to work out exactly how this could have happened accidentally, but that was his story. Later he went back on it and denied knowing anything at all about Hogan. It wasn't a convincing denial though – her head had been in a paper sack in his house.3

Given what had been found it was obvious that Gein needed psychological tests, and the result was no surprise – he was unfit to stand trial for the murder of Bernice Worden. The psychologists did manage to get some insight into what had driven him though. Fixated on his mother, he'd never had a relationship of any kind with a woman. Thanks to Augusta's crazed teachings Gein had believed that men were all irredeemable sinners while women were the source of goodness, and probably he'd concluded that the only way to become a better person was to become female. Certainly he denied any sexual motive in his theft of stealing so many female corpses; he denied having molested any of them, adding that "they smelled too bad."[4] Matter of fact statements like that were common during the interviews. Gein seemed to have no idea of how appalling his crimes had been. It was obvious to the psychiatrists that he was completely psychotic and had no understanding of right or wrong. The community of Plainfield wanted him tried for Worden's murder, but there was no hope of a successful prosecution. Instead he was committed to the Central State Hospital for the Criminally Insane, a grim red brick institution in Waupun.

As Gein's notoriety spread a flood of murder aficionados descended on Plainfields, eager to see the scene of the atrocities. The old farmhouse became a monument to murder, much to the disgust of local residents. The sheriff's department had to step in when the company hired to dispose of Ed's belongings tried to charge an entrance fee to view them. Finally the house caught fire early on March 20,

1958 and rapidly burned to the ground, ending any chance of it being exploited as a museum. When Gein was told of the fire he said, "Just as well." His remaining possessions – some farm equipment, his 1949 Ford – were auctioned off, with the car ending up as a carny sideshow attraction for a quarter a look.

That car might have deeper significance to the Ed Gein case. The only clue remaining from the disappearance of Georgia Weckler, the eight-year-old who vanished on the way home from school in 1947, was a set of tire tracks found near the spot where she had last been seen. They were carefully analyzed during the investigation for any clues about what model of car they belonged to. Detectives concluded that the mystery car had been a Ford.

[4]
THINKING ABOUT NORMAN

Robert Albert Bloch was born in Chicago on April 5, 1917. Like Ed Gein he was descended from German immigrants, in his case Jewish ones. When he was ten he managed to get into a late-night movie on his own; it was Lon Chaney, Sr.'s Phantom of the Opera and it scared him half out of his wits. From then on he had a deep interest in the horror genre and soon started writing his own macabre tales. When he was twelve his father lost his job and the family moved to Milwaukee, where his mother worked in a community center for the local Jewish community. More importantly for

Robert he started attending Lincoln High School, which had an active literary magazine. Robert soon befriended the magazine's editor, Harold Gauer, who turned into a lifelong friend. Bloch showed some of his writing to Gauer, who then published one of them in the magazine.

In the 1930s America had a huge range of fiction magazines covering every genre you could think of. One of the most popular was Weird Tales, which focused on stories of horror and the supernatural. A frequent contributor was H.P. Lovecraft, and Bloch, with his interest in horror, quickly became a fan of Lovecraft's tales of ancient, hungry monsters. In 1933 he wrote the author a fan letter, and Lovecraft replied with advice and encouragement. The teenager's circle of contacts quickly grew to include some of Lovecraft's friends, and his talented but amateurish fiction improved rapidly under their guidance. In early 1934 he had a story published in a minor magazine, Marvel Tales, which attracted some interest. That July he sold two stories to Weird Tales itself, the first of which was published in November.

More success followed; he began to write stories set in Lovecraft's Cthulu Mythos, often expanding the mythical universe to do so. One story featured a character based on Lovecraft himself, who (with the author's permission) died horribly in the course of it. Lovecraft responded by dedicating his next story to the young writer – the only time he ever added a dedication – and basing a character (who, of course, died horribly) on Bloch. Over the next two years the pair developed a close friendship and their works interacted with each other in a darkly humorous way.

In March 1937 Lovecraft died of cancer aged only 46, his last written work a diary in which he recorded, with gruesome enthusiasm, every detail of his illness. His death was a serious blow to Bloch but he didn't let it affect his work. He did open up the scope of his writing beyond the Cthulu genre but remained firmly in the realm of horror. By the early 1940s the subject of serial killers was starting to interest him. In 1943 Weird Tales published Yours Truly, Jack the Ripper, which featured the Victorian killer as a supernatural being who had to kill to sustain eternal life. In 1945 Lovecraft's old publisher released Bloch's first book, a collection of short stories titled The Opener of the Way. Combined with a radio production of Yours Truly it gave Bloch's career a massive boost. His first novel, The Scarf, was published in 1947. The villain is a serial killer who preys on women.

When Ed Gein was arrested in November 1957 Bloch was living less than 30 miles away in Weyauwega. The case made the local news and Bloch quickly became aware of it. He didn't bother to do any extensive research into it or follow later developments, but it did start him thinking. What struck him was how utterly unaware the people of Plainfield had been. After Gein's arrest they were almost universally stunned at what had been going on for years, practically under their noses. Plainfield was a small town, with barely 800 residents; how could a local man have gone so horribly wrong without anyone noticing? Small towns are famous for their gossip and the difficulty of maintaining privacy, after all, so how had Gein done it?

Bloch started to reflect on the idea of the hidden depths that can pass unnoticed even in a close community. We all think we know our neighbors, he mused, but how well do we know them really?

Bloch's idea was to write about someone who was in the public eye, well known and apparently respectable, but who secretly led a much darker existence. He chose as his antagonist a motel owner – someone who's constantly dealing with the public but turns out to be showing a façade with no resemblance to the real personality beneath.

Psycho was published in 1959 and caused a sensation in the psychological horror market. It opens with a woman traveller, Mary Crane, who checks into the isolated Bates Motel. She interrupts an argument between the proprietor, Norman Bates, and his elderly mother. Bates sees that she is exhausted and invites her to have dinner with him at his house. Shortly afterwards Mary hears Norman tell his mother about the invitation; she screams a vicious threat.

After dinner Mary is showering when she is attacked and beheaded. Norman finds her body and deduces that his mother was responsible; he considers letting her face the consequences but changes his mind and conceals the corpse.

Mary's sister Lila visits her boyfriend Sam Loomis to tell her that she had vanished. Planning a search for her, they are soon found by Milton Arbogast, a private detective who is also looking for Mary. They agree that Arbogast should lead the search. He begins to track her movements and the trail leads him to the Bates Motel. Norman tells him that Mary stayed for one night and then moved on. Arbogast then asks to speak to Norman's mother, but he refuses. Suspicious, Arbogast phones Lila and says he plans to try to speak to Mrs. Bates.

Arbogast manages to enter the Bates house and begins searching the rooms. Then suddenly a strange figure – the same one that killed Mary – attacks him with a straight razor.

With Arborgast also missing, Sam and Lila head for the Bates Motel to investigate. The local sheriff is surprised to hear that Arborgast wanted to talk to Mrs. Bates; he reveals that she killed her lover and herself years ago. Norman found the bodies and was so traumatized he spent time in a mental hospital. Puzzled by this story, Lila and Sam go to the motel. They become suspicious at Norman's behavior and Sam keeps him talking while discreetly sending Lila to get the sheriff. Instead she decides to explore the Bates house. As she does so Norman tells Sam that she has tricked him and gone to the house, where his mother will kill her. Sam tries to go after her but Norman knocks him out with a bottle.

Lila, investigating the house, finds the mummified corpse of Mrs. Bates. Moments later Norman rushes in, dressed as his mother, and attempts to kill her. Sam, who has recovered and followed Norman to the house, overpowers him.

At the end it is revealed that Norman, driven insane with jealousy when his mother started a relationship, had murdered her and her lover with poison then forged a suicide note. Mentally breaking down, he had convinced himself that she was still alive. Stealing her corpse he preserved it in the house, and whenever his illusion was shaken he dressed in her clothes and talked to himself in her voice. The delusion went so far that his personality split, and the "mother" half continued to dominate him as his real mother had.

When Bloch wrote his novel he was only aware of the rough outlines of the Gein case. Later, when he learned the details, he confessed to being astonished at how closely the real killer had matched Norman Bates.

[5]
Challenging Hollywood

Alfred Hitchcock had had a successful run of movies in the 1950s, but as the decade drew to a close he was having some issues with Paramount Pictures. His last two projects, Flamingo Feather and No Bail for the Judge, had fallen through - the latter because female star Audrey Hepburn had become pregnant - and he was looking for a dramatic idea that would restore his lead in the face of competition from other directors.

Hitchcock was usually reluctant to accept plot ideas provided by studios; he preferred to rely on his own inspiration and suggestions provided by a few trusted advisers. One of these was his filming assistant, Peggy Robertson. Like Hitchcock Robertson was a fan of a Sunday column in the New York Times, a book review section that specialized in mysteries. It was written by Anthony Boucher, who also wrote as H.H. Holmes (a name he took from a 19th century serial killer). One of the books Boucher reviewed was Psycho. Robertson passed the review on to Hitchcock, who immediately ordered a copy of the novel. It didn't take him long to decide that here was the plot for his next feature.

At this stage more problems emerged. The novel had already been read by researchers at both Paramount and Universal, who'd been interested in its potential for a screen adaptation. Now Hitchcock approached Paramount with his idea, only to be told that they had already ruled out filming Psycho. It wasn't suitable material, they told him. The sexual and violent content was unacceptable to them.5 In any case audiences wouldn't want to see such a disturbing story.

Hitchcock had his own opinions about that, and he was determined to make the movie.

Paramount was equally determined not to, though, and the director was tied into a contract with them that committed him to making one more film. He began negotiating with the studio, trying to find a solution that would let him go ahead with filming. Paramount was adamant, though; they couldn't stop him doing it, but they wouldn't give him any support – or money. Hitchcock countered, offering to film it on a budget. He proposed using his TV production crew, who worked with him on Alfred Hitchcock Presents, and shooting the movie in black and white to keep costs down. Paramount still wouldn't agree to finance the project and claimed that all their sound stages were booked solid, even though the movie industry was going through a dry spell at the time.

Finally Hitchcock offered to finance the movie himself and shoot it with his own crew, using the sound stages at Universal, if Paramount handled distribution when it was finished. Instead of his usual director's fee – which at the time was $250,000 – he would settle for

60% of the takings. Paramount, who didn't expect the movie to earn much, finally agreed.

It wasn't just Paramount that was skeptical about the project. Hitchcock's own film crew was organized as a company called Shamley Productions, named after the English village of Shamley Green where Hitchcock owned a country house.6 Joan Harrison, an English producer who served as an executive with Shamley and had been working with Hitchcock since 1933,7 agreed with the studio that the project wouldn't be a commercial success. Another Shamley producer, Herbert Coleman, agreed. Hitchcock rode over their objections and started pulling the strands of the project together. As well as his determination to see the movie produced there was also an element of curiosity involved. The big Hollywood studios might be reluctant to film sex and violence, but some of the smaller independents had no such scruples. In the late 1950s there were an increasing number of low-budget horror movies, usually with very low production values. Now Hitchcock had a chance to show how well a low-budget title could be done.

[6]
CREATING THE PLOT

The first stage in developing the movie was the screenplay. Hitchcock turned this task over to James P. Cavanagh, who produced a draft. It wasn't what the director was looking for, however. He felt it was more suitable for a TV mystery show, which probably wasn't surprising given that Cavanagh normally wrote episodes for Alfred Hitchcock Presents, and that it didn't have enough suspense and horror. Then he was approached by Joseph Stefano, a former pop music composer who'd only written one screenplay before. He'd recently been taken on by 20th Century Fox and now his agent wanted to know what his next project would be. Stefano, who had a lively sense of humor, handed over a list of the ten leading directors in Hollywood and told the agent to contact them, but not to bother Stefano with their replies unless one of them had a job waiting. He was astonished when he got a reply from Hitchcock.

Despite Stefano's relative inexperience Hitchcock decided to give him a try – after all the one script he'd written so far had ended up starring Anthony Quinn and Sophia Loren.8 In fact Loren had won the Best Actress award at the Venice film festival on the back of that movie, so it wasn't as much of a risk as it might have seemed.9 There was another shock waiting for Stefano though. The writer was excited at the idea of working on one of Hitchcock's famous dramas; now he was handed a gory horror paperback and told to adapt it.

Stefano decided right away that some changes had to be made. Movie audiences develop empathy for characters in a different way from readers, and Stefano felt that if Mary

Crane simply appeared, stopped at the Bates Motel and was almost immediately killed audiences wouldn't actually care much. He developed a sub-plot in which she steals $40,000 from her boss then goes on the run with the money. During a conversation with Norman Bates her conscience tells her to return the cash, and she has just resolved to do so when she is killed. That gave the audience time to get to know the character, so her death had more impact.

He also changed the character of Norman himself. In the novel he's a pretty degenerate figure, a middle-aged alcoholic who collects pornography and peeks at female guests for thrills. Stefano turned him into a younger and basically likeable character.

Other scenes were added too, most significantly one showing Mary and Sam in bed together. This was to cause controversy later. Most of the other changes were minor, and aimed at building suspense more effectively on screen. The plot followed Bloch's fairly closely, even if the dialogue and scene details had been extensively reworked.

After some minor adjustments Hitchcock was satisfied with Stefano's screenplay and turned to the issue of casting. He suggested Janet Leigh to play the part of Mary– he also directed that her name be changed to Marion, after discovering that a real woman named Mary Crane lived in Phoenix.10 Leigh was a big name at the time, and casting her would be a big boost for the movie's appeal. The death of the female lead barely 45 minutes into the film would also be a major shock to the audience. Stefano wasn't sure about Leigh as he felt she had "no association" with this type of film, but in fact she had played a similar role in the 1958 Orson Welles thriller Touch of Evil.11 She was also enthusiastic; in fact after reading the novel she agreed to take part without even asking Hitchcock what her fee would be (it was $25,000 – a quarter of what she usually got from Paramount.)

With Bates now depicted as a less overtly deranged character than in the novel, Hitchcock decided on Anthony Perkins to take that part. Still in his late 20s, Perkins had a pleasant and youthful look that exactly suited Stefano's image of Norman. He also had the talent to play the role – he'd been nominated for an Academy award in 1956 and had starred opposite Jane Fonda and Sophia Loren.

Although Leigh, as Marion, was the most prominent actress in the script the female who actually spent most time on screen would be her sister Lila. Hitchcock wanted someone talented and reliable for that part, and he turned to Vera Miles. The 30-year-old Miles had worked with him before, playing the wife of an unjustly accused musician in the 1956 docudrama The Wrong man.

John Gavin, a relatively new actor who was being groomed as a male lead by Universal, was chosen to play Sam Loomis. Gavin – who was later considered to play James Bond – would make a sympathetic character, but wasn't prominent enough to overshadow Perkins and Miles.

The cast list fitted Hitchcock's aims perfectly. Without Paramount's support his budget was limited to what he could raise himself, and he was also becoming increasingly frustrated with some of the major Hollywood stars. High fees could swallow huge chunks of a movie's budget and some of them felt secure enough to make excessive demands as a condition for appearing. One of Hitchcock's preoccupations around this time was to build a group of actors and actresses who had the talent he was looking for but weren't powerful enough to insist on changes in the script to suit their self-image. The ensemble he had now put together met those standards. Now it was time to start filming.

[7]
Shooting Begins

With Paramount's movie sound stages unavailable, Hitchcock fell back on the resources he used for his TV show. Revue Productions had been set up by MCA as a radio studio in 1943 and expanded into television in 1950. By 1960 it was part of the Universal group and Alfred Hitchcock Presents had become one of its most popular shows. Because most of the shots for Psycho would be interiors it had the facilities he needed. Another advantage was that he could tightly control access, which would help in keeping details of the plot out of the Hollywood press.12 Hitchcock sent researchers out to find the sort of locations that would be portrayed in the movie – real estate offices, motel rooms and suburban homes – and take hundreds of photographs. This was typical of his attention to detail, allowing the set designers to capture the feel of a real location. He even identified a woman similar to his image of Lila Crane and had her entire collection of clothing photographed. There would be no ordinary woman with a catwalk wardrobe here – Lila would be wearing authentic outfits.

Most of the crew for Psycho was taken directly from Alfred Hitchcock Presents. Hitchcock already knew them and they were familiar with how he worked, which would make life easier on set. Some key specialists were brought in from outside, mostly people he had worked with on previous movies. One of these was Bernard Hermann, who had written most of the music for his films. George Tomasini had edited seven Hitchcock productions since 1954 including North by Northwest and the classic murder thriller Rear Window.13 Finally designer Saul Bass was hired to produce the storyboards and title sequences.

One of the most iconic images from Psycho is the Bates house itself. Rambling, rickety and sinister, it looms above the motel and some of the most dramatic scenes take place in and around it. Inspiration for its appearance came from a painting by Edward Hopper, a realist artist who specialized in scenes of ordinary American life. His oil painting The House by the Railroad showed a three-story timber frame house with a large veranda and neo-Gothic tower, and Hitchcock decided to emulate its look for the movie.14

While the sets for the house and motel were being constructed Hitchcock began work on location shots. One of his technical aims was to beat a shot filmed two years earlier by Orson Welles, one of his main rivals among Hollywood directors. In Touch of Evil Welles opened the movie with a long "dolly shot," a sweeping scene through a town where the camera traveled several hundred yards on a crane-mounted platform. It was an impressive piece of camerawork and Hitchcock had been pondering ways to top it. The solution he hit on was to use a helicopter. His vision was for a scene where the camera crosses a town and finally zooms in on a hotel window, through which Sam and Marion can be seen in bed together. If it all worked as intended the shot would cover an incredible four miles, easily surpassing what Welles had achieved.

As it turned out filming from a helicopter isn't as simple as it looks. Helicopters are notorious for vibration, and until the development of stabilized camera mounts filming from them was an extremely hit and miss process. Sections of the shot were too shaky to be used and it had to be spliced with studio footage. While it didn't quite achieve Hitchcock's aim of getting one up on Welles the long sweep, from the Phoenix skyline down to the window, did work as a dramatic piece of cinema.

As well as high-profile scenes like this a huge array of stock and background footage was needed. Early in the movie Marion sets off from Phoenix in her car, on the journey that will ultimately end at the Bates Motel. For the scenes of her driving highway footage was needed, which would then be added as a background using the bluescreen technique. A crew filmed it along Highway 99 between Fresno and Bakersfield, using a California location because it was more convenient for the Universal lot in Los Angeles where the production was based. Location shots for the scene where a highway policeman finds Marion sleeping in her car were also taken at the same time.

Other filming continued in Phoenix, including street scenes. When the footage from one shot was examined Hitchcock realized that Christmas decorations could be seen in some of the stores. Rather than have it reshot he simply had an appropriate date – December 11 – added to the opening titles.

Finally the sets were ready at the Universal lot and the bulk of the shooting could begin. Although his crew normally worked on his TV show Alfred Hitchcock Presents was shot using standard movie camera equipment, which was also used for Psycho. The 35mm cameras were fitted with 50mm lenses instead of the short telephoto lenses normally preferred for movie production. The 50mm optics have a similar visual field to the human eye, which gave the movie a more intimate look.

That would greatly increase the atmosphere of indoor scenes. Where shooting took place outside the standard lenses, with a focal length of 80mm or more, were often used.

Instead of rigidly scripting the shots Hitchcock decided to let the stars improvise their scenes. That had some amusing consequences. In the finished movie Norman is often seen eating candy corn, a quirk introduced by Perkins.

Hitchcock had his own quirks, of course. In 39 of his 52 surviving feature films he appears in a cameo role. This quickly became a popular feature of his work and fans would eagerly watch for a glimpse of the director. In fact it became so popular that he began to introduce the cameos close to the beginning of the movie, so that audiences wouldn't be too busy looking for him to spot vital elements of the plot. For his Psycho appearance he decided to play up a family connection. Hitchcock's daughter Patricia was an actress, and as well as frequent roles on Alfred Hitchcock Presents had previously appeared in three movies (two of them, Stage Fright and Strangers on a Train, directed by her father.) In Psycho she was cast as Marion's work friend Caroline.15 To get himself in a shot with her, while not being too obtrusive, he stood outside the window of the office wearing a Stetson hat while Leigh and Patricia chatted inside.

Of course Psycho was filmed from start to finish with Hitchcock's usual care and attention, but one will always stand out in the memory of everyone who's ever seen it. That's the infamous shower scene, and getting it right would become one of the most grueling technical challenges of his long career.

[8]

Creating the Horror

In Bloch's novel the shower scene is brief and comes to an abrupt end that's as matter of fact as it is gruesome – "It was the knife that cut off her scream. And her head." Hitchcock planned to use it to build up tension on its way to a shocking climax, and that was going to take every ounce of compositional skill he had.

The shower scene is a complex mixture of multiple viewpoints, some of which had technical difficulties of their own. For example one shot looks directly at the showerhead, with jets of water flowing all around the camera. If water had actually hit the lens it would have distorted the image beyond usability, so the shot had to be carefully staged. The center nozzles of the shower were blocked and the camera was fitted with a telephoto lens; although it looks as if the camera is close to the shower it was some distance away and the streams of water had diverged to pass well clear of it.

Another concern was to minimize the amount of nudity in the scene. The fact she was in the shower obviously meant Marion would be naked, but there was a limit to the amount of flesh that could be revealed without falling foul of the censors. Breasts, for example, needed to be avoided. The initial shots were easy enough – Leigh was either filmed with the shot cut off at her upper chest, or seen through the semi-opaque shower curtain. The actual attack was trickier though; the curtain was out the way and Hitchcock wanted to show Marion cowering away from the repeated blows of the knife. That needed careful coordination of the camera and Leigh's movements. It also needed numerous retakes. Hitchcock always avoided retakes wherever possible, believing that the first performance of a scene was likely to be the freshest and most natural. In fact in many of his movies he had the rehearsals filmed and often used that footage, with the "official" shots kept as a backup.

It didn't work out that way for the shower scene. From the moment Marion drops her robe and steps into the shower to the point where the camera pans away from her dead face is only two minutes and 43 seconds, but filming it took a week. Two cameras were used, one of them a handheld model that could be used for awkward close-ups.

As well as keeping Leigh's noticeable charms out of the frame there were also difficulties with the end of the scene, when the camera lingers on her face as she lies on the floor. In the finished shot Leigh's pupils are contracted to tiny points, a natural reaction to the bright lighting. In reality a dead person's pupils dilate to their full size.[16] Hitchcock considered using contact lenses to give this appearance but rejected the idea. Contact lens technology was a lot more primitive than it is now, and before wearing the lenses for an extended time Leigh would have had to acclimatize herself to them. That would have taken up to six weeks, an unacceptable delay.

Other factors made the scene a tricky one. Dead people don't react to what's happening around them, but Leigh kept responding to the water that splashed into her face. There was nothing that could be done about that; it's a reflex action and can't be controlled. The only solution was to shoot that sequence over and over again until they got it right.

In total the shower scene was made up of over 50 separate shots, an average of barely more than three seconds each – and many of them were much shorter than that. Stitching them together into the finished sequence was a long and demanding process. Every take of every shot had to be carefully examined for continuity errors, unwanted movements and breasts, graded for suitability then used or discarded. The assembled footage had to be coordinated with Herrmann's atmospherically Wagnerian score, which played a huge part in the finished scene. In fact Hitchcock originally wanted to show the shower scene without music, but Herrmann insisted. When the director saw the result he immediately doubled Herrmann's fee.

Even with all the effort that went in, a glitch nearly slipped through to the final print. Luckily Hitchcock's wife, Alma Reville, made a habit of checking all his work before release. Reville was an assistant director and film editor, who'd met Hitchcock when they both worked at a London studio in the 1920s. She was credited on many of his later movies, and while she wasn't officially credited as having worked on Psycho she took a close interest in its production. The fact that Hitchcock had mortgaged their home to help raise the funding for it may have given her an incentive to pay attention to every detail. In any case she realized that in the final shot of Marion lying dead on the floor it was possible to see her breathing.17 There wasn't a lot of time to sort this problem, because it was one of the final viewings before release, but Hitchcock managed to edit the negatives in time.

The filming of the shower sequence managed to cause a controversy decades after

Psycho was released. Both Hitchcock and Leigh were adamant that no body double had been used, and that Leigh had shot all the scenes herself. No member of the crew has ever mentioned a body double. However a 2010 book by author Robert Graysmith claims that in fact many of the shots in the shower were of Marli Renfro, a soft porn model who Graysmith admits to having been obsessed with since seeing her in Playboy in 1960.18 In fact Renfro, who was approximately the same build as Leigh, was hired to double for the scene in which Norman carries Marion's plastic-wrapped body to the trunk of her car. Graysmith didn't know that fact in 1960, when he promised himself that one day he would write a book about the "unique, unforgettable" redhead stripper19 with the "indefinable quality" that fascinated him.

    Graysmith seems to have become confused by 2001 newspaper reports of an old murder, although in his defense he wasn't the only one. Leigh had had a stand-in for the movie, Myra Davis. The stand-in's job was to take Leigh's place while shots were being set up, allowing the crew to check lighting and sound levels without having expensive stars on set. Davis was raped and strangled in 1988, and when her killer was caught and convicted thirteen years later some papers inaccurately reported her as having been Leigh's body double. Graysmith initially thought that Myra Davis had been Renfro's real name, but then discovered that the 63-year-old Renfro was still alive and living in California.20 In his book he argues that Davis's killer, handyman Kenneth Dean Hunt, was an obsessive Psycho fan who had wanted to kill Leigh's body double out of jealousy but messed up and murdered the stand-in.

Whoever the body was in the shower – and Leigh said many times that it was her – the overall effect was a shocking one. When analyzed frame by frame surprisingly little is revealed, but it's so well cut and edited that the minds of the audience take a rapid-fire succession of images and build them into a hideously detailed picture of a brutal murder. Even simple touches like Marion's blood flowing down the drain – chocolate syrup was used because it shows up better on black and white film – were cleverly arranged to heighten the atmosphere.

Two more myths have grown up around the shower scene. One is that it was actually directed by Saul Bass, the graphic designer. Bass claimed this in the 1990s, but it was refuted by Leigh and assistant director Hilton Green. It seems unlikely that Hitchcock, known for his perfectionism and the rigid control he demanded over every detail of the production process, would have handed such a vital scene over to someone who wasn't even a trained director. Finally, it's often rumored that to make Leigh's screams more realistic cold water was sprayed on her through the shower. Leigh denied that too, saying that the crew was always very good at making sure she had hot water.

[9]
Reception

Psycho was released on June 16, 1960 under extremely strict conditions. Hitchcock insisted that the stars gave no interviews before the release, in case they gave away the twists of the plot. That might seem pointless for a film based on a novel that had been on sale for a year, but there are persistent rumors that Hitchcock had tracked down and bought almost every copy of the book to preserve its secrets as much as possible. Advance screenings for film critics were dropped, which displeased the critics (and attracted some mediocre reviews) but prevented leaks. Most controversially of all Hitchcock ordered theater owners not to let anyone in after the movie had started. There were protests at this, as some were worried that this would cost them business, but in the end Hitchcock was proved right. The air of mystery that built up around Psycho ensured that on opening night many movie theaters had queues around the block. It went on to bring in over $60 million at the box office, and was so successful that it was re-released in 1965. It first appeared on TV in 1967 and has been reshown frequently ever since. It's still guaranteed to draw good ratings.

If movie audiences loved Psycho, film censors weren't so sure. The American film industry at the time was ruled by the iron restrictions of the Motion Picture Production Code, a set of guidelines that laid down what was acceptable. Adopted in 1930, the Production Code was based on the earlier work of a Presbyterian elder, Will H. Hays, and was predictably stern on matters of "immorality." It included a long list of things that could not be depicted on film, including interracial relationships, homosexuality, a long list of expletives, adultery and prostitution. Any crimes shown in a movie had to be punished and it was forbidden to portray them in a way that might seem sympathetic to the criminals. Sex outside of marriage could not be shown in a positive light and authority figures had to be treated with respect. The clergy could not be shown as either comic figures or wrongdoers under any circumstances, although police officers could be on occasions. Even by the standards of the 1930s the Code was incredibly strict; worryingly it actually discussed the need to prevent "thought crime" nearly two decades before George Orwell made the term famous in Nineteen Eighty-Four.

    The Production Code was a relic of the era that gave the USA Prohibition, and by the late 1950s it was attracting increasing derision. American audiences were crowding into theaters to see foreign productions that openly flouted the Code. Breasts were unthinkable in a Hollywood movie but in an Italian one they would pass unnoticed (by the Italian censors at least – perhaps less so by US audiences.) Independents also regularly broke its restrictions, and with the studios banned by antitrust laws from owning movie theaters there was a growing market for taboo films.

The Code had been drawn up at the request of studios and was enforced by them; it had no legal backing. Because Hitchcock was working more or less on his own with Psycho he decided to push the boundaries and see what he could get away with. He didn't push them too far, of course – he wanted Paramount's distribution network on his side – but the Code was definitely creaking under the strain and Hitchcock knew it. The extra stress of Psycho started to break it to pieces, and it was finally replaced with the MPAA rating system in 1968.

The first issue with the Production Code enforcers was the scene early in the movie showing Marion and Sam in bed together. Although Leigh was wearing a brassiere in a small concession to decency, some of Paramount's Code censors claimed they could see a bare breast. Hitchcock knew they couldn't, because there wasn't one, but he also knew there was no point arguing with Hollywood's self-appointed moral guardians. Instead he told them he'd reshoot the scene. A few days later he handed them the exact same print for review. This time the censors who'd seen the breast before didn't, while those who hadn't did. The scene passed.

Incredibly, the other major objection – even more troubling to the Code department than the shower scene - was the sight of Marion flushing a torn-up letter down the toilet.21 No flushing toilet had even been shown in an American movie before and the thought of allowing this scene left the censors extremely disturbed. It's not quite clear what they thought they were protecting the American public from – most people who went to the movies no doubt had a flush toilet of their very own – but they were still reluctant to give it the all clear. Only Hitchcock's persuasiveness got it into the final release. That was just as well, because it was vital to the plot; a piece of the letter that didn't flush away becomes a clue about Marion's disappearance.

Conclusion

By the time Hitchcock made Psycho his reputation as one of the greatest filmmakers of the 20th century was already secure. Perhaps that's what made him do it, because it was very different from the suspense movies he'd built his career on. Psycho, although it used suspense very effectively, was a slasher pic at heart. Its huge commercial success changed the way Hollywood saw sex and violence and hastened the collapse of the restrictive Production Code. Most of the horror movies made today owe their existence to Psycho.

What did Psycho do for its production team and stars? All four of the main players continued successful acting careers, and Perkins in particular received a huge boost from the publicity of his role as Norman Bates. For Hitchcock it was an artistic triumph and a financial windfall – the huge takings made his 60% share far in excess of the normal fee Paramount had denied him. It didn't mark a significant change in artistic direction for him – his next movie, The Birds, was another horror, but after that he returned to psychological dramas with Marnie. He must have wondered sometimes though, because nothing he made later came close to Psycho's commercial success.

Psycho has to be counted a success for the people who made it and, although many of them didn't want to believe so at the time, for the American film industry. By helping give studios back the freedom to compete with foreign movies it opened the way for Hollywood to produce content geared to different audiences rather than the draconian, one size fits all restrictions of the Production Code. What about audiences though? By modern standards the actual violence in the film is incredibly restrained, but the artistry behind it means it's still consistently rated as one of the best horror movies of all time. Perhaps because its production ruffled so many feathers in the movie industry it didn't get the recognition it deserved at the time – nominated for four Academy awards, including Best Director and Best Supporting Actress (for Leigh) it didn't win any of them, although Leigh got the same award from the Golden Globes and the Edgar Allen Poe awards rated it Best Motion Picture.

Of course none of that is the recognition that really matters. Even today, more than half a century after that shower curtain first jerked back to reveal Norman in his mother's clothes, Psycho still does what Hitchcock intended it to do. It makes people scream.

READY FOR MORE?

We hope you enjoyed reading this series. If you are ready to read similar stories, check out other books in the *Stranger Than Fiction* series:

THE TRUE STORY BEHIND ALFRED HITCHCOCK'S THE BIRDS

The Birds was different from most of Hitchcock's work. For admirers of Hitchcock The Birds also raises disturbing questions about the director as a person. He was a complex and confusing character in many ways, and perhaps it's not surprising that someone who built a career out of creating suspense and fear on screen might also have had some darker sides to his personal life.

Beyond the details of the story and how it came to be filmed, though, one of the most interesting questions about The Birds is why Hitchcock made it in the first place. It took its title from a short story by English author Daphne du Maurier, but beyond the basic idea of people being attacked by birds it didn't take much else from it. The storyline was pure Hitchcock. So where did it come from?

It turns out that his inspiration was a strange and alarming incident that happened just a few miles from his home in California. This book uncovers the truth behind the plot as well as other factoids that fascinate any fan of the film.

Exposing Jack the Stripper: A Biography of the Worst Serial Killer You've Probably Never Heard Of

Jack the Ripper may get all the fame, but his 1960s counterpart, Jack the Stripper, will really send shivers down your spine. At least six women, all prostitutes, were murdered at his hand--possibly more. Most intriguing of all...he was never caught.

The crimes, though often forgotten today, inspired the crime novel "Goodbye Piccadilly, Farewell Leicester Square," which Alfred Hitchcock turned into the 1972 movie, "Frenzy."

Go inside the hunt for this brutal killer in this gripping short biography.

The Sapphire Affair: The True Story Behind Alfred Hitchcock's Topaz

In October 1962 it looked to millions of people like the politicians of the United States and Russia were determined to push the other across the fatal line of launching a nuclear strike. The fate of the world hung on Cuba, a troubled island state in the Caribbean.

Woven through the dramatic events in and around Cuba was a quieter but perhaps equally dangerous scandal – an enormous, deeply embedded network of Soviet spies at the heart of the NATO alliance.

A senior KGB defector had revealed that his agency had penetrated the highest levels of the French government, military and intelligence services – but when a French agent tried to act he found himself blocked at every turn by his own superiors.

Alfred Hitchcock was so impressed by the fictional novel about the events (Topaz by Leon Uris) that he decided to adapt it into a movie. But fiction, as is often the case, only got half of the story. This book tells the remarkable true account of one of the greatest espionage scandals to rock the Cold War.

THE PERFECT CRIME: THE REAL LIFE CRIME THAT INSPIRED HITCHCOCK'S ROPE

Leopold and Loeb were two wealthy law students who could buy anything. But they wanted the one thing that no amount of money could buy: life. They wanted to create the Perfect Crime--to kidnap and murder a 14-year-old boy for the thrill of getting away with murder.

The crime was so horrifying that even legendary filmmaker Alfred Hitchcock took notice and directed his version of the story: Rope. But the real story of the Rope is much more brutal and suspenseful than even Hitchcock could do justice to. Read the real history in this thrilling true crime book.

THE TRUE STORY BEHIND ALFRED HITCHCOCK'S THE WRONG MAN

The Wrong Man tells the incredible tale of an innocent man falsely accused of a crime. That in itself is hardly an unusual story, but in this case a string of unlikely coincidences and sheer bad luck built a seemingly airtight case against him. It seemed that the entire justice system was deaf to his pleas and all too willing to ignore the evidence his defenders had worked so hard to unearth. In the end it was only a slip by the real perpetrator that proved his innocence.

While the movie certainly had it's share of truth, it was still a movie, and parts were fabricated. This book tells the real story behind the movie.

Newsletter Offer

Don't forget to sign up for your newsletter to grab your free book:

http://www.absolutecrime.com/newsletter

Notes

[1] Crime Library, *Eddie Gein* p2
http://www.trutv.com/library/crime/serial_killers/notorious/gein/begin_2.html

[2] Schlechter, Harold, 1998, *Deviant: The Shocking True Story of Ed Gein*, pp.30-31

[3] Gollmer, Robert H., 1981, *Edward Gein*, p.22

[4] Crime Library, *Eddie Gein* p.1
http://www.trutv.com/library/crime/serial_killers/notorious/gein/bill_1.html

[5] Classic Movies, *Alfred Hitchcock's Psycho*
http://classicfilm.about.com/od/mysteryandsuspense/fr/Alfred-Hitchcock-S-Pyscho.htm

[6] Hitchcockwiki, *Shamley Productions*
http://www.hitchcockwiki.com/wiki/Shamley_Productions

[7] The New York Times, Aug 25, 1994, *Joan Harrison, A Screenwriter And Producer, Is Dead at 82*
http://www.nytimes.com/1994/08/25/obituaries/joan-harrison-a-screenwriter-and-producer-is-dead-at-83.html

[8] The New York Times, Aug 31, 2006, *Joseph Stefano, 84, Screenwriter for 'Psycho' and Television, Dies*
http://www.nytimes.com/2006/08/31/obituaries/31stefano.html?pagewanted=print&_r=1&

[9] The Washington Post, Aug 30, 2006, *Joseph Stefano; Key Writer for 'Psycho'*
http://www.washingtonpost.com/wp-dyn/content/article/2006/08/29/AR2006082901421.html

[10] Leigh, Janet and Nickens, C, 1996; *Psycho: Behind The Scenes of the Classic Thriller* p.23

[11] Bright Lights Film Journal, *Touch of Psycho?*

http://brightlightsfilm.com/14/psycho.php#.UuPbpbQwdaQ

[12] Cinefantastique, Oct 28, 2010, *Stephen Rebello on Psycho*
http://cinefantastiqueonline.com/2010/10/author-stephen-rebello-on-the-making-of-psycho-a-celebration-of-1960-retrospective/

[13] Motion Picture Editor's Guild, *An Interview With Mary Tomasini*
http://www.editorsguild.com/v2/magazine/newsletter/directory/tomasini.html

[14] Wagstaff, Sheena, 2004; *Edward Hopper*, p.234

[15] IMDB, *Caroline (Character) from Psycho* http://www.imdb.com/character/ch0003074/?ref_=nm_flmg_act_4

[16] Right Diagnosis, *Dilated Pupils*

http://www.rightdiagnosis.com/d/dilated_pupils/intro.htm

[17] Universal Studios, 1997, *The Making of Psycho* (Documentary)

[18] Los Angeles Times, Mar 23, 2010, *The Girl in Alfred Hitchcock's Shower, by Robert Graysmith*

http://articles.latimes.com/2010/mar/23/entertainment/la-et-book23-2010mar23

[19] IMDB, *Marli Renfro* http://www.imdb.com/name/nm0719505/?ref_=ttfc_fc_cr71

[20] The Guardian, Mar 29, 2010, *Secrets of the Psycho shower*
http://www.theguardian.com/film/2010/mar/29/psycho-body-double-marli-renfro

[21] The Guardian, Oct 22, 2010, *Psycho: the best horror film of all time*
http://www.theguardian.com/film/2010/oct/22/psycho-horror-hitchcock

www.ingramcontent.com/pod-product-compliance
Lightning Source LLC
Chambersburg PA
CBHW020301030426
42336CB00010B/862